from the hill of the Wild Berries

New writing from
County Wexford

Edited by Sylvia Cullen
Foreword by Billy Roche

Published by
Wexford County Council © October 2008

The Arts Department
Wexford County Council
County Hall
Wexford

Tel: +353 53 76500 Fax: +353 53 43532
Email: arts@wexfordcoco.ie
www.wexford.ie

ISBN: 978-0-9549165-5-8

Edited by Sylvia Cullen

British Library Cataloguing in Publication Data. A CIP catalogue record for this book is available from the British Library.

Design & layout by karen nolan design, www.karennolandesign.ie
Printed in Avenir 11pt
Printed in Ireland by Colour Books

Ceramic pot in cover artwork created by Tom Lawlor of K.T.A.C.
Ink drawings contributed by: Billy Doyle, Martin Freeman and Billy Glanville from Killagoley Training & Activation Centre (K.T.A.C.)

Contents

Introduction

We need to give each other the space to grow, to be ourselves, to exercise our diversity. We need to give each other space so that we may both give and receive such beautiful things as ideas, openness, dignity, joy, healing, and inclusion.

Max de Pree

Arts Ability was initiated by the Arts Department of Wexford County Council during 2003, with the aim of celebrating the creative imagination of people who experience mental health problems / disabilities and providing inclusive opportunities for equality of access to the arts. Over the past five years, *Arts Ability* has undoubtedly had a significant impact on enhancing the quality of life of its participants, and in doing so, has directly met Wexford County Council's overall mission.

Inclusive arts practice is based on the principle of involving people with disabilities as artists, participants and audience members, in addition to creating an environment in which people from a range of backgrounds can work together as creative equals where learning is possible for everyone. *Arts Ability* is a very fine example of this model, in which the voice and ability of everyone is valued and nurtured on an individual and equal basis.

The success of the *Arts Ability* creative writing programme at K.T.A.C. has been very much due to the unconditional commitment of the participant writers, the enthusiastic support of all staff and the vision of Sylvia Cullen in nurturing creativity and inspiring previously untapped imagination. On behalf of Wexford County Council, sincere congratulations must go to all involved.

Eddie Breen
County Manager

Councillor Peter Byrne
Chairman
Wexford County Council

Introduction

Everyone has their story. For each it is unique and reflects something special that stays with the mind, shining with a comfortable glow long after the circumstances that gave rise to it. This collection of writings is a collection of individual stories that give us an insight into the uniqueness of each author and impresses again and again. The collection emphasises the wonderfully creative nature of us all and is a reassuring reminder that despite adversity, each of us has a wonderfully creative ability.

Wexford Mental Health Services has been fortunate to have had the opportunity to work in partnership with Wexford County Council and the Arts Council, as part of *Arts Ability*. Through this programme and the enthusiasm of the participating writers and artists, we witness the great benefit that creative imagination can bring to our wellbeing. Particular praise must go to all involved, most especially the individual writers and artists themselves, as well as the artists-in-residence whose energies have enabled these storytellers and inspired them on their journey.

Kevin J. Plunkett
Director of Nursing
Wexford Mental Health Service

Preface

Killagoley Training & Activation Centre was born out of the amalgamation of the Industrial Therapy Unit and the Skillbase Unit in January 2005 and it now caters for thirty-three service users on a daily basis, Monday to Friday, all year round.

The Industrial Therapy Unit was a workshop setting; it was the brainchild of Joseph Casey, Chief Nursing Officer at St. Senan's Hospital in 1982, who had the foresight to see the advantages of such a unit. Service users carried out a number of different tasks, all very meaningful in their own way. Contract work such as making bed sheets and repairing furniture for local hospitals, were some of the tasks that were carried out. The Industrial Therapy Unit was managed by Wexford Mental Health Association for the South Eastern Health Board and this partnership proved very fruitful for all involved.

The Skillbase Unit was set up in 1990 to cater for service users who did not wish to get involved in a workshop, but wanted a structure to their day. It offered a rehabilitation and training programme to people with mental health problems and encouraged them to look honestly at themselves and recognise their strong points and build on these.

Killagoley Training & Activation Centre (K.T.A.C.) offers the opportunity to relearn and develop skills, to acquire some new skills, in order that service users will be able to enjoy a better quality of life and leisure, with renewed confidence in themselves.

The creative writing sessions show that there is so much more to people than we see on the surface, their stories revealing different aspects of their experiences, as well as their talent. It is very difficult to put into words what the writing of this book has meant to the authors; it has offered a whole new outlet and a welcome diversion from other battles and difficulties of day to day living with mental health problems.

Finally, I would like to acknowledge the contribution of the Arts Department of Wexford County Council along with the Arts Council and the Health Service Executive who funded the *Arts Ability* programme. Thanks also to Wexford Mental Health Association for their kind support down through the years. I wish to express my gratitude to Sylvia Cullen, Writer-in-Residence, who managed the production of this collection with a lot of dedication and commitment. Special thanks to Liz Quill for all her hard work and enthusiasm for this publication, and to all the staff of K.T.A.C.

It has been a pleasure to be associated with this anthology and I hope it brings many hours of enjoyment to all.

Pat Murphy
Manager
Killagoley Training & Activation Centre

A Word from the Editor

What is it about the blank page?... What is it that makes it so inviting, yet simultaneously so utterly intimidating? How is it that the act of taking up a pen to write, arouses so many conflicting emotions and offers so many tantalising options?

Tuesday became Creative Writing Day at Killagoley and for the last three years, the long room where we worked was transformed and took on the ambiance of a creative cell: most days it went very quiet and if you interrupted us, all you'd see was heads bent, all you'd hear was pages turning, books being consulted and the scratching sound of pens. People writing in longhand holding pens to their heads, their hearts, their ears, their lips... All patiently putting words on paper, scribbling out their stories as they saw fit.

On other days you might surprise us in the middle of a Nigerian storytelling session, or a swopping of Spanish folktales; you could catch us debating the twist in a short film, or silently sitting, all ears, while Shakespeare or Wordsworth or Kavanagh was quoted from memory. Of course there were many days spent looking out the window for inspiration; frustrating afternoons trying to make the words fit, foosthering, fiddling and being downright finicky.

The work that has evolved out of those sessions has an intimate, authentic quality, which comes from long percolation by people who trusted and took the leap of faith required for this particular artistic journey.

For those of us who have worked together over the past three years, *From the Hill of the Wild Berries* represents a hugely satisfying step. Seeing the work of all these writers in print, gives me great pride and a huge sense of achievement. It is with enormous pleasure that I introduce these distinctive and original new voices to you, the reader. It has been a privilege to work with the storytellers of Killagoley and I wish to thank each and every one of them for three wonderful, rewarding and most enjoyable years.

Sylvia Cullen

Foreword

'Only that which is glimpsed sideways sinks deep' is the old writing adage, and the writers and poets in this anthology seem to know and obey that rule instinctively. Insight and wisdom are to be found here if the reader looks close enough, like the sun skimming across a wild berry hill on a cloudy day.

In a story called *Cowboys* by Paddy Galvin, the writer lets us feel what it might be like to be a lonely cowboy, washing his clothes in a river and hanging them to dry on a nearby tree, worrying about wolves and swimming in the cool, clean water, unaware that a few Indian lads are creeping through the field to watch the cowboy floating. On the face of it it's a simple tale, simply told, but underneath there is a beautiful metaphor for the worries and sad cares of all our lives.

In yet another story called *Shaving*, Martin Freeman reminds us that there was a time when we could tell a lot by the look of a man's beard: a moustache meant a financial wizard, a goatee spelt out the Water Service while sideburns seemed to suggest rock and roll. Now the writer mourns the fact that we must all sit in some fancy hairdresser's chair and just take our chances with the rest of them.

On the other hand *Ritual*, by Sarah Tuomey basks in the beauty of a mother and daughter as they share in the everyday, almost holy ritual of making themselves up.

And in the lovely poem *X* by John Yates when a girl says that life is a game the poet very wisely assures us that whatever else it is, life is not a game. This poem is a true work of art.

And the night is not always tender
And the day is not always hard...

which in anybody's language is a beautiful turn of phrase.

I'd like to extend my warmest wishes to all the writers and poets and their mentors who were involved in this project - my brothers and sisters-in-arms! The stories and poems I mention are just a sample. There are many more where these came from, poems and stories glimpsed through the frosted glass of troubled lives lived. So please read and enjoy and be prepared to gasp at the hidden glittering gems that lie at the heart of this collection.

Billy Roche

Acknowledgements

Grateful acknowledgement is made to Wexford County Council, the Arts Council and the H.S.E. who funded the *Arts Ability* Creative Writing Residency. An especially warm thank you to everyone at the Arts Department of Wexford County Council for all the advice and assistance over the last three years.

Thanks are also due to Billy Roche for his foreword and Anne Doyle who launched the publication. To Heather Deacon-Rothwell, Artist-in-Residence, St. Senan's Hospital and all of the other *Arts Ability* artists and host organisations, for their help and encouragement.

Grateful thanks to Wexford Mental Health Association for their generous contribution to *Arts Ability* over the past five years.

Hugh Kelly deserves special mention for bringing the poetry of Pat Rossiter to my attention, as does Cyril Fenlon who suggested the title for the book. Wood Hill of the Wild Berries is the original translation of Vinegar Hill - *Cnoc Fiodh na gCaor*.

As well as thanking all of the staff working at K.T.A.C., I would particularly like to acknowledge the immense contribution of Pat Murphy and Liz Quill, whose unstinting support in so many ways, made the creation of this book possible. The work of all of the writers is acknowledged in the introductions and the labours of the Book Committee - John Yates, Mary B. Keyes, Noel Galavan and Moira Naessens - on behalf of all the contributors, is especially appreciated.

Sylvia Cullen

Monologues

Penned In

Michelle Cullen

Being a prisoner is no fun. My cell is so miniscule, I feel claustrophobic. I barely have enough room to stand up. The cells are very dark and there's a funny smell. Outside, written on the wall is -

SILENCE

there's to be no communication between any of us inmates.

I've witnessed people being hanged here. A friend of mine, Peter Kehoe, was hanged in the yard. My own crime was assault - I attacked an old woman just to get a few pounds off her. Five years I was given - I suppose it wasn't bad given the nature of my crime.

At night-time you can hear the rats scurrying around the cells. I'm afraid to eat any of the food left into us, in case of Weil's disease. But there again, if I don't eat the food, I'll starve...

My personal hygiene is poor as the prison cells lack washing facilities. If I spend much more time here, I'm terrified my spirit will be broken. Five years is a long time to be penned in. Please God I'll be released soon.

Vivien Leigh has One of Those Days

Sarah Tuomey

I had an awful day today. I woke up late and realised that I forgot to take my tablets the previous evening. Arriving on the set of *Gone with the Wind*, I was a bit cantankerous. I hadn't memorised my words either. It was just one of those days that used to always happen to me.

Gone with the Wind is an important film that I am making. It might break or make me. My mental illness has prevented me from coming to my fullness as an actress, with mood swings, feeling up, feeling down, facial contortions, changes in my tone of voice and so on.

My co-star, Clark Gable who plays Rhett Butler, was a big help to me and indeed a good friend. Our friendship never frayed despite my ill health. Due to my illness, we had to shoot certain scenes a couple of times, in particular the one at the door when he says 'Frankly my dear, I don't give a damn!'

My illness used to cause me to cry a lot and that was particularly bad when I had my studio make-up on - the mascara and the heavy foundation running in rivulets down my cheeks. The make-up artists had to re-paint my face a few times.

After finishing on set today, I returned home after a hard day's work. I threw myself down on the bed, closed my eyes and rested - sleep to cure and heal my weary head. As I nodded off, I dreamed of my part in the film and hoped to win that much coveted Oscar.

Maybe

E. C.

I'm worn out today. Exhausted.
Wouldn't want to get out of the bed.
I'm fed up painting.
What's the point in me working when no one
wants my paintings?

My head is like a cement mixer. I feel like dying.
I'm not even going to open the curtains.
I want my tea in bed today.
Nothing much.
Just a cup of hot tea and a ham sandwich.

(Van Gogh twists in the bed.)

I'd just like to see a light at the end of the tunnel.
I don't want to see them days again, days when I'm
really depressed...

(He turns over, thinking of the colours in his paintbox.)

Maybe I will get out and do a bit after all.
I'd like to paint that field of golden barley outside.
And the black crows flying around,
All excited 'cos they're going to get a feed.

My Name is Josie

Tony Allen

My name is Josie O'Farrell. Myself and my young grandchildren are tenants on a crop of land. It's the famine years and I worry about them every day - that they will have enough to eat and good clean water to drink.

Their parents died of fever and starvation. My eldest son James and his good wife, Anne. They left two adorable children behind: John and Kate.

The three of us never have enough to eat. The children are going around in rags. John tries very hard to pull vegetables out of the earth. We never have meat unless sometimes we catch a rabbit and cook up a stew. More times than not we don't have anything at all to eat...

The landlord is going to evict us and I don't know what the little ones are going to do. I wish times would get better but I'm not going to give up yet. God will surely protect us.

The Pain of Confinement

Sarah Tuomey

Locked in my prison cell.
All my freedom taken from me.
Broke the law - robbed a bank with some pals.
Guards were called and a high-speed chase ensued...

The judge and the jury put the blame on me - Guilty! -
Got seven years.

The jingle-jangle of the prison warden's keys, when the door to my cell is opened in the morning.
Sit to eat breakfast - prison food - slop!
It's a bit like bread and water.

Return to the cell and while away the hours reading.
Have things to occupy ourselves - woodwork, classes in engineering...
The day is long - night falls, go to sleep early - dream.
Dream a bit like *Escape from Alcatraz*!

Next morning - next day - back to the old slog.

Cigarettes are a scarce commodity in prison.
The warden rations them out to us - you'd be dying for a decent fag.
Miss home - Da, Ma, all the family.
Visiting hours are something to look forward to.
Not too long.
Talk to my parents and brothers and sisters,
Across the open counter.

Poetry

Watches

Bridget Murphy

It's a curious thing that watches have faces,
Like us.
Watches don't talk.
Don't cry.
Don't smile.
Don't get cross.
They never wash their glassy face.

Nuns

Bridget Murphy

They can't smoke.
They mustn't curse.
They shouldn't go with men.

Some had to get their hair shaved off,
Years ago. But not now.

They are supposed to wear a habit and veil,
And bring invalids to Lourdes.

I would like and love to be a nun myself,
Because they have time to pray.
What I wouldn't enjoy is kneeling on a boarded floor,
Getting a pain in the bones of my two bare knees.

Thinking About Nothing

Margaret Kehoe

Cigarette memories.
Nice.. Sweet.. Heavy.. Heavenly.
The taste of white smoke in your mouth.

My favourite cigarette is *Benson & Hedges.*
I like them best.
I enjoy them.
Better to smoke inside than out.
You think about nothing. Standing there.

When I was a young girl, you could buy cigarettes singly.
I was twelve when Mammy used to buy them for me.
Taller than me with her brown, curled hair,
Mammy, standing there, not minding.

Me?
I'd slowly smoke and smile, feeling better.
Flicking back my long, straight hair.

The Pheasant

Margaret Kehoe

Lately I saw one walking in a wood,
Searching for barley to eat.
Moving slowly, looking all around,
Trying to look behind with wide eyes.
Afraid of the sound of a gun.
Worried about the smell of a fox.
Nervously scratching and rooting in the leaves.

Now the hunter runs it into a corner.
Traps it. There's no escape.
Poor pheasant feeling scared and snared.
He's going to be shot – he'll end up on the kitchen table,
Only to be eaten by the hungry farmer.

Tastes like good meat between his teeth.

Hand Speech

Michael Carroll

When I'm not at ease,
Communication feels tougher.
Stress makes it twice as tough.
Communicating with each other through movement,
Reduces all that stress.
It doesn't feel as tough when I move while I speak.
Pressure.
I was pressurising myself into wanting to get out to people,
What it would be like to be able to speak at ease.
I was making myself suffer.
Getting stressed up!
However... When I move from the hand,
I find myself better able to find the words I was looking for.
Movement can make the difference.

Communicating

Michael Carroll

Conveying your feelings,
Announcing your plans,
Revealing your secrets,
Divulging your dreams,
Expressing your emotions.

It's a question of finding the right pace.

Not too fast, not too slow.
We're caught in between.
Need to learn to do our
Speaking without talking.

Glendalough

Orla Slevin

A blue cast over the grey mountains.
Neat stonework on the tall round tower.
The lovely lakes that surround Glendalough
Are like tin foil reflecting the clouds and ash trees.

It was grand and peaceful strolling through the grounds.
I was happy in myself and at ease with nature.
Despite the good crowd, I was relaxed and refreshed,
My thoughts turning to Saint Kevin.

My Master's Degree

Barry Mitten

I tried but failed my Master's Degree.
I tried several methods of passing this.
I would go to the chemist for my tablets.
I would try to cash my grant at *Barclays Bank*.
I would cook my own meals,
And would go to the shop for myself.
But I never passed my Master's Further Degree...

An Awakening of Nature

Michael Bolger

Spring is a new beginning.
Foxes awaken to life in Spring.
The leaves on the Oak tree are green
and give a fresh atmosphere to Spring Life.
The swallows return from foreign lands
to the pleasant island of Ireland.

The yellow daffodils are bright and blooming.
The mornings are precious with the beautiful
sound of different birds singing.
The beauty of the afternoons is followed
by the bright evenings,
Which resemble a new scent of life.

Farmers feel the sweat on their brow after ploughing the land,
And sowing and spraying corn.
Their preparation for the harvest begins in earnest.
People of all professions are carefully
planning their summer holidays.
The lack of the Spring Show is evident in Ballsbridge...

The caterpillar changing to the butterfly, which is a fresh start,
Is almost equivalent to Spring.

Youghal

Moira Naessens

Hot sand beneath our toes.
Sun beaming on our heads.
Crowds down on the beach.
Red sunburn on their backs, legs and bodies.

Colourful bikinis on girls, size twelve, fourteen and sixteen.
Pink with envy...
Blaring rock 'n roll radios.
Screams for Joe "Isn't he gorgeous? What a swimmer!"

Smell of coffee from the restaurants.
Lovely salad sandwiches.
Candy floss melting in our mouths.
Classy clothes in shops.

Sun going down.
Time to go home.

Summertime

Michelle Cullen

Today is a beautiful day,
The rain is kept at bay.
Sun's high in the sky,
Summer's here – that's no lie.
Children playing at sea,
At their parents' mercy.
Flowers are in full bloom,
The sky's so clear - at night you can see the full moon.
So have no fear - Summer's here.

The Crow

Andy Donohoe

The Crow is flying on sad thoughts today.
It's hard to know why,
But he's able to take you out of trouble.

Singing

Michael Kinsella

A good singer holds his head up,
And sings out loud and clear.
His voice good and strong,
Carrying right to the back of the hall.
He needs to take a big long breath,
Deep. Filling his lungs with clean air.
Then he opens his lips wide,
Ready to sing like a lark.

What Happened to Christmas?

Larry Connick

What happened to Christmas?
It went dead.
And why?

These times it's something like May or June.
It doesn't snow or freeze or blow.
No frost nor snowflakes.

Still alive is it?
Should've went dead...

Bell Tone

E. Ryan

The Friary Chapel bells are damaged.
I believe a crack has appeared.
Years ago, the Friars would sound out a certain bell tone,
To let the people of the town know they were short of food.

Sadly now, since the bells were damaged,
They no longer sound.

The Sedative

Pat Rossiter

I see their eyes and face.
They look at me,
Staring beyond me, calculating.
There isn't a comment,
Just their ice-cube eyes,
Melting into my mind.
Now I see the bed, white sheets.
I, like some sort of sandwich between them,
Waiting to be swallowed into
A vacuum of confusion.
Then the syringe
The sharp steel ready
To stab into my existence.
It happens, the surgical spirits,
The movement, the sting,
The chemical pulsating into my brain.
The mind staggers beneath reality,
Rainbows weep from the electric light.
I lie there, locked in prescribed mind cuffs.
It doesn't make sense, no meaning a threat,
The rainbows staining my thoughts
As colourful as darkness.

The Effects of the Effects

Pat Rossiter

The spiders pulled their silver nets,
Through an ocean in my mind,
And purple fish swim from my eyes,
Leaving golden scales behind.

And the shadow that stood upon the floor,
Became a beaming light.
On monkey's legs it walked away,
And vanished out of sight.

The curtains swayed, then fell like glass,
And sparked upon the floor,
And darkness staggered through the window,
In volume never seen before.

I shouted words, but they just froze,
Suspended in the air.
Then a tin soldier came to me,
And tied chains on to my hair.

The electric bulb became a blood drop,
And my vision then turns red,
The blood like a shadow of an escaping dream,
Was seeping out of my head.

I was coming back, my room seemed pale,
Then the chains fell from my hair.
Reality then set me free,
From a place, I don't know where.

The Sinking Miracle

Pat Rossiter

The setting sun raised her shadow on the wall.
From her wheelchair she observed
The sinking miracle falling into darkness.
For thirty years she hadn't left her house,
Except when her imagination escaped
To the meadows of her youth.
Monthly, a pale-faced priest
Paid a discount on her fare to Heaven.
Her eyes were like mirrors
Reflecting endurance.
Yet, there was always room on her face
For a smile.
Her tears often washed a frown from her face.
She liked the night,
The darkness kept her company,
A playground for her thoughts.

Be

William Hayden

Be Quiet
Be Friendly
Be Honest
Be Unique
Be Careful
Be Truthful
Be Humble
Be Yourself

Curracloe Beach

Maureen O'Connor

It was one dark, dreary day,
I wandered down the lovely, sandy beach.
The waves were rushing to and fro.
I heard a sort of squealing noise up in the sky...
And what was it?
Only about five or six big seagulls,
And as I kept on walking,
The waves seemed to get stronger and stronger.
And then I told myself: Maureen, it's time you took off home!

Late Bloomers

Claire Tuomey

It was a day that could have been torn from a child's
colouring book.
Bright autumnal sun wafting through the trees.
Birds tweet-tweeting and the faint scent of summer
everywhere.
Camellias and hibiscus in late bloom and rhododendron
flowers blowing in the breeze.
The leaves of an old oak tree turning russet brown.
A season in decline.
They say that once the leaves turn in Ireland, the winter is
upon us.

And nothing's left to chance.
The logs are cut for the hearth and the sou'westers bought
for the night chill.
The evening's mood is enhanced by storytelling and poetry
reading,
To warm the heart and lighten the soul.

In this Northern Hemisphere,
Seasons turn in the blink of an eye,
But the flowers bloom again in the spring.

The Tramp

Claire Tuomey

The winter nights are closing in around us.
Stars showing in sparkling bunches between drifting clouds.
Small sounds, sighing winds.
Black boughs creaking in the silence.
Rutted fields laid bare, dark and waiting,
Where an old tramp sleeps.
His nest a ruins of a plastic bag, full of
Cigarette ends and dried, dead leaves as his bed.
No home, no comforts.
With the sullen sky as his only blanket.
A shambling, untidy figure will emerge from this bed in the morn,
To fumble in the dustbins of household refuse.
A person can be glad of their comfortable bed,
As the winter nights close in around them.

Emergency Room

Claire Tuomey

One dead baby, a dying cousin, a universal uniting of grief.
The grieving more intense because of the death of the child.
Perhaps wrong on the sorrow level for the death of innocence versus maturity,
Though everybody grieves in their own way.
The desperate parents hollow-eyed and entwined,
Are still in the waiting room.
One sombre nurse arrives to fetch them
And I hear the agonising loss of a high-pitched wail from the corridor.
There are more people bustling to the monitoring machine.
Is this the end?
Pale, greenish lights move across the screen in regular spasms.
There was no private goodbye.
I disconnect the machine and the pulsing lines straighten.
Whatever had been in the quiet body is no longer there.

Rockpool

John Yates

Nestling in the rocks at St. Helen's
There is a rockpool.
This microcosm of existence
Is cosseted by sea and air.
Cobalt and azure blues play patterns on the water
And the sky is reflected on the pool's surface
As it gently laps the weedy edges.
Momentarily a small beetle rises
The circular ring of the ripple barely perceptible
Before it descends again to its hide.
If you entered the pool barefoot
An unseen crab might nip your toe
And the feel of the bottom might be slippery or slimey.
It depends on sea and tide to refresh.
We all depend on refreshment.

The Last Bathers

John Yates

The calm of the evening.
The beach on its own.
The water quiescent and still.
But no,
I can see heads bobbing
And the top of a torso.
They break the surface
But do not splash.
Sound does not drift over
From their place of play.
A swim at day's end
Enjoying the sea warmth retained.
Are our generation
The last bathers?

X

John Yates

Trickle the tears down my cheek
Enliven my life with smiles.
The seesaw goes on and on
Ups and downs, downs and ups,
And I don't always crave balance.
I am alive at moments of extreme,
But there is pleasure in sleep too,
And happiness has its own serenity.

Cloud patterns in the sky sometimes attract our attention.
On a clear night the stars are always there,
But we only occasionally look up at them.
A full moon casts a shimmering light,
Some stars are brighter than others.
For each of us some people are special,
And the night is not always tender,
And the day is not always hard.

So let the dealer give out the cards
And we'll play our hands as best we can.
But when a girl said, Life's a game,
I said, Whatever it is, it's not a game.
Maybe it's a seesaw,
Fun on a fine day
With someone nice at the other end,
Up, down, in balance.

Prose

Myles Doyle's Shop

Christy Doyle

When he looks out, he can see the whole town,
Because he's up on a hill.
He can see the far side of the road,
See cars, tractors, lorries, motorbikes.
See the pedestrians; see who his next customer is...
Mister Myles Doyle, Gorey shopkeeper supreme.
It's his habit to wear a white shop coat.
He's a short man, not very tall; has a good friendly manner
And keeps everything tidy and neat.
Shelves stacked high with brown and white bread,
All different kinds of home-made jam: berries, apple jelly, sweet marmalade...
Keeps a bacon slicer up on the counter.
No papers nor sweets, but French and Spanish wine...
He has a lot of chat for the customers,
Would talk about the hurling, football and the weather.
He's from Craanford and follows the local team.
A jolly-going man, he's used to standing all day long.
Opens at nine, half-five closes.
I've known him these years.
He'll probably work right up to the end.
Happy out.

Rathgarogue School

Larry Connick

It's out by Ballywilliam, on the way to Ross. Between there and Rathnure. I didn't learn that much, though I got through the letters a bit.

Three classrooms was in it. All had blackboards. A whole lot of presses full of books and writing. Lovely white toilets as well. Special wooden desks to sit at with benches joined on that lifted up and down. Small little yards outside for kicking around football or rugby.

I was age four when I first went into it. On that very first day there were birds going around. I had a whole lot of brothers: two older and two younger. Gussie brought me but he was in a different room, in with the Master. Boys and girls were in the one room together.

Eileen and Emily Greene were the schoolteachers. Both kind and gentle. Young and healthy. One of them, Eileen, she had green eyes and talked a lot. Arrived to work in a brand new brown Opel.

Emily was my first schoolteacher ever: Red hair. Calm. Clever.
I remember being taught about Noah's Ark.

It's a long length ago now.

My Happy Memories

Cyril Fenlon

I remember the day my first baby girl was born in Wexford Hospital. We called her Mary-Louise. At that time in my life, we were all into soccer - football - and my favourite player was George Best. So, as Mary-Louise was growing up, I used to play football with her in the garden. I even used to call her Georgie and eventually we re-named her Georgina. Everyone knew her by 'George' and it suited her perfectly.

She was born during the summer of 1976. Looking back, I can remember she was long and thinnish, with very little hair - although she has a right crop of it now.

Later on, I was allowed to be at the birth of my fourth child and I remember that very well. Another girl – Jessica. They dressed me up in all this white gear and I was like a spaceman going into her. I remember catching my wife Patricia by the two wrists and the nurses were all shouting 'Push, push!' and I remember hearing myself say 'Push, Push PUSH!' And then 'Push be fuck!' When suddenly, out she popped.

It was brilliant - I'll never forget it. They wrapped her up in a little white sheet and I held her and she was beautiful and still is. My little girl let a roar out of her - God I thought there was something wrong. It was a powerful cry, a real babby's bawl. And Jessica is still going strong to this day. And to this day, she can still let a good screech!

Patrick

Kieran Sinnott

My uncle is a plasterer and I used to work with him. He was like a Dad to me. We'd have a good laugh together at work. We even used to think the same way about other people. The reason I liked working with him is because we were on the same level about things.

My job was mixing the cement. There are ten shovels of cement in a bag and you mix it four to one: four shovels full of sand to one shovel of cement. You add water until the mix is soft and creamy. With a cement mixer, this only takes ten minutes. Then you put it on a mortarboard and the plasterers plaster the outside walls with it.

Patrick, my uncle, had blue eyes and black, straight hair. He was a small, blocky man who had a bit of a temper. When things went wrong on him, the temper would come out of his mouth.

On the way home from work at the weekend, he used to pay me my wages and used to bring me to the pub to buy me a couple of drinks. One thing he hated was listening to the radio when he was working. He'd rather be whistling or singing to himself.

The Story about Willie

Kieran Sinnott

I see him every morning in *Skillbase*. We drink coffee together and smoke a few cigarettes. Most days we talk about money, the weather and people we both know.

He's a good friend and we know each other for fifteen or sixteen years. Sometimes he gives me cigarettes and I do the same for him. Other times he cheers me up. With his funny sense of humour, he makes me see the lighter side of life.

Another side to this man is that he is a good listener. I trust him because he can keep a secret. As there is an age difference between us, I love to listen to his entertaining stories about when he was younger and used to work in a shoe shop, fitting on other people's shoes. He also tells great tales about his working life in England. He makes me laugh with his yarns about going to dances at Irish Clubs with his brother and his friends.

Another factor in our friendship is that we live fairly near one another. We know the same villages and some of the same characters. I used to visit him in his mobile home years ago. Willie is easy to talk to and great to listen to.

The Barge Factory

Tom Lawlor

The Barge Factory was a business in New Ross. I started with the company when I was about thirty years of age. I remember my first day at work when I had to fill up a form to get hired. John Kent was Personnel Officer there, looking after about two hundred people working in the factory.

I was doing general work where there was a lot of welding going on. I would erect scaffolding for the men to weld. It is easy to get a flash if you look at welding in progress. It feels like sand in your eyes - uncomfortable.

We used to do shift work from eight in the morning 'til four in the afternoon and from four to around twelve at night. It was nice to get home around midnight. Some days I got a lift into work with a neighbour and the odd time I brought my own transport.

The wages were very good - up to two hundred pounds a week. We used to get paid on a Friday and I saved up a lot of money.

The barges we made were transported to the Lebanon. I never travelled on one myself but some of the foremen would stay on the barge and sail on it, to test it out.

At the moment there is little going on at the factory site.

St. Senan's Farm

Tom Lawlor

James Hendrick is steward on the farm at St. Senan's Hospital where we had fifteen acres of spuds each year. At the moment the farm is closed down.

We used to start in the morning about nine o'clock. Half a dozen of us would go to the spud field. We worked with a blue chain digger: it is used to take out the headlands and then we changed to a red potato harvester.

We had two tractors drawing metal trailers. Each trailer would carry three tons of potatoes. The two very popular varieties were Cara and Rooster.

I really enjoyed this work because there would be five or six of us boys working together in a cluster. It was a little bit tiring standing most of the time. Sometimes you would bend one knee to get a break. It was good to be kept busy.

Sometimes the crows used to be lighting on the spuds, looking in the fresh clay for worms. Later on at the dinner, if we were having beef stew, we would enjoy freshly picked potatoes with it.

Lotto Luck

Moira Naessens

One evening after work, I bought three scratch cards.
My heart started to beat...
I won fifty euro.
I yelled for joy!
It was Friday evening and the shops were open.
I went into the jeans shop and I bought with the money,
A pair of 501 *Levis* jeans.
They fitted comfortably.
The price of them was forty euro.
I was pleased.
I went home strolling.
My Mum was in the house.
'Guess what Mum? I won fifty euro and with the
money I bought a pair of blue *Levis* jeans!'
My Mum turned to me and said:
'Congratulations Moira - boys are you lucky!'

The Return of Pusskins

Kirsten Sellhorn

At the beginning of September 2004, three kittens were abandoned at the I.T. unit at Killagoley. Pat Murphy and I looked after them till they were old enough to go to homes.

A F.E.T.A.C. tutor took two kittens and the smallest one came to us in Moran Park, supposedly as a housecat. He was called Pusskins. He was quite good but also a bit bold, although he was clean and very neat about eating. He used to do a little bit of biting and scratching, mostly in play.

But one day, I came home and he had bitten one of the residents quite badly. A tetanus injection had to be given and there was quite a commotion. We decided he had better live outside. There was an empty coal shed in the back where I put jumpers and left the door ajar so that he could come and go as he pleased. I was quite worried because he was only five months old...

It didn't really work out because he was afraid when the heating boiler was buzzing and so I tried to keep him in my room for a few hours every day. Then, one day, soon after Pusskins was put out, he was gone. I was very upset and thought that was it, our precocious kitten is gone.

On the third morning after he went missing, I was making porridge for my breakfast when I heard a meowing outside the back door. I opened it and there was Pusskins with his tail up!

I couldn't believe it. I rushed to get some cat food and surprise, surprise; he walked into the shed, even though the heating was on. I looked at him eating for a while, then I started to get ready for work.

All's well that ends well. He did disappear again a second time, but that's another story...

Elf

Kirsten Sellhorn

I left school very young, at fourteen or fifteen and went as a working pupil on a stud farm owned by Mrs Hall-Dare. It was near New Ross at a place called Ballykerogue. Mrs Hall-Dare owned quite a few ponies and horses. She also had hens, cats and terriers. I remember one of the ponies - she was called Elf.

Elf was pretty. She was quite big, fourteen hands, but she was also dainty. She was black with a white blaze and white socks. Mrs Hall-Dare bred ponies mostly. When they were trained and proven to be quiet and used to some equestrian activities, they were sold.

I used to exercise Elf every day. When she was trained she was a pleasure to handle. In the winter, I had to go hunting with Elf a few times, which sometimes quietens ponies and they get used to company and learn to jump. I am against fox hunting but it was part of my work and I wasn't quite as sensible then as I am now. I hunted several seasons and fortunately a fox was never caught.

In the summer, I rode Elf at the pony club and Mrs Hall-Dare was beginning to look out for a suitable buyer. Before a new home was found, I was asked to ride her in a show which made me very nervous. I think the show was in Ballycogley.

I groomed her as well as I could that morning, plaiting her mane and tail and putting oil on her hooves. I thought she looked lovely and shiny but I was still feeling nervous myself. We got to the show and I couldn't even eat my lunch...

When we were called, I was still nervous. As I rode

around the ring, a sheepdog jumped in front of Elf and I fell off near the judges. The amazing thing was we still won the show and even more amazing was we won overall championship and one of the judges told Mrs Hall-Dare and I, that Elf had to get the award because she looked so well. We were delighted and soon after, Elf was sold to someone who was going to bring her to England.

I was sad for a while but there were a lot of other animals that needed looking after and hopefully she went to a good home that gave her plenty of love and attention.

The Prisoner

Michael Bolger

It was 1798 and John was a Pikeman. He had killed an English soldier and was sentenced to death by hanging. He had to stay in a prison cell for six months before that dreaded day.

To John, every day seemed like a month: he had nothing to do except to look out the barred window onto the back yard where he was going to be hanged. All John had to look forward to was a miserly mug of water at half-eight in the morning and a few slices of bread at one o'clock.

The so-called bed he slept on, was made of timber with a pillow and case but no mattress. Even during the day, the prisoner spent hours lying on the bed, but because of his future death (which was coming nearer day by day) John found it impossible to sleep. Even at night he found it difficult.

Now, it was the night before his execution and he was, understandably, awake all night. The hanging was to take place at ten a.m. At 9.45 the guard brought the prisoner out to the yard, still wearing handcuffs. John chose to have his face covered so he couldn't see anything. Suddenly he felt the rope being put around his neck. He felt the trapdoor giving way and the rope tightening. He felt the knot pressing hard against his Adam's apple and then he died.

The River

Michael Bolger

The river is beautiful in the morning.
While standing under the trees, one can get a glimpse
of the sun shining on the water, which is uplifting.
When fishermen catch a rare sight of fish jumping, it is
exhilarating and exciting.

One can't help but admire the trickle of tiny waves, which
resemble miniature horses swimming on the river.
Children bathing in the water is a joyous occasion.
Whilst waiting patiently on the bank, fishermen are eagerly
anticipating catching a fish.
Minnows swimming together are meat for bigger fish.

When walking by the river, it is easy to admire the wonderful
sight of river animals like otters.
The cob and the pen swimming with their young cygnets are
a pleasure to behold because they are a beautiful example
of nature.
The wondrous sight of trees like alder, and flowers like water
lilies,
Birds like herons, dippers and kingfishers, can stimulate one's
imagination.
One can't help but feel sorry for the fish when hooked by
fishermen and the frantic struggle which follows, until the fish
is reeled in and either killed or released back into the river.

A Difficult Day for Charles Dickens

Michael Bolger

Charles Dickens woke up at seven a.m. on a Monday
morning.
He had hoped to complete that precious story *Oliver Twist*.
But his depression was unbearable that morning.
So he went for a six-mile walk in the hope that his
bad mood would pass.
He arrived back to his house at about one p.m. and felt a
lot better.
Then he took his medication and had dinner.
After this meal, his head was a lot clearer.
So he was very well inspired to finish the uplifting story of
Oliver Twist, a mix of violent characters and the innocence
of the child.

Ritual

Sarah Tuomey

Grace was first introduced to make-up, face creams, fashionable clothes et al, by her mother, Maisie. Mothers, young and old, often show off their children - particularly if they are beautiful.

Rummaging around her mother's room, Grace found her first bottle of foundation - an old, much used, worn out jar of *Revlon*. She had learned how to apply make-up from watching Maisie.

Reasonably priced clothes were bought in local stores and both Grace and Maisie liked to dress up. Hair was another important feature: shampooed, cut, washed and blow-dried, once a week to once a month. Magazines helped, advising them on all the latest trends in hairstyles, fashion, make-up and creams.

As they grew older together, these beauty routines all became an important ritual for the two women.

A Photo Finish

Gerald Morrin

A photo finish is defined in my dictionary as 'end of a race in which a camera is used to determine the winner'. This is followed by a semi-colon and the second and final definition given is 'very close finish'.

On the twenty-third of September 1959 in the final of the Grand Prize at Enniscorthy Greyhound Racing Track, a photo was called for as the result of the race was a very close finish indeed and the winner could not be declared by the naked eye. The Grand Prize was the premier event of the year at the track and, even at that time, must have been worth about seven hundred pounds sterling to the winning owner. The runner-up would receive about one hundred and fifty pounds so the stakes were high.

My uncle Mark had greyhound kennels at Woodlands and in the 1959 season, his hopes rested on *Cherry Rocket*. The training season started with us at the beginning of the school holidays i.e. early June and it would take about six or seven weeks to bring a greyhound to racing fitness, so that a hound would be fit come St. Swithin's Day, July 15th. We had always wanted to win the Grand Prize. There were two methods of entering a dog in this stake; the dog could qualify for entry by winning or coming second in a Grand Prize Qualifying Race of which there would be many during July. Alternatively, the dog could be entered by paying the entry fee which was about ten pounds sterling. There would be seventy-two dogs or bitches competing at the start and this would be whittled down to six qualifying for the final as the stake progressed and the first and second round heats and semi-finals were run off.

Our hope had qualified for entry by winning a Grand Prize Qualifying Race in late July and after the stake started in August, he won his heats in the first and second rounds and came second in the semi-final, which was good enough to qualify for the final. My uncle, who owned the dog and who had been associated with greyhounds for over forty years, was not a betting man; that is, he did not gamble a lot or heavily. But when his own dog was running with a chance, he might place a small wager say twenty pounds or even a pony (twenty-five pounds) on him. Sometimes it was possible to bring off a 'coup' and get a wager on at a good price, say 6/1 or 7/1 with the bookies and, if the dog won, the rewards could be quite substantial.

The notion of bringing off such a coup appealed strongly to my uncle who reckoned that the bookmakers made a good living from gambling. The methods used to bring it about were all legal and above board. At all costs, the dog must not be favourite but must be an outsider. To become an outsider meant that he must not have won his heats too spectacularly or in an exceptionally good time. In greyhound racing the form of a dog is forecast by his time in previous races. If a hound has won his heats with ever-improving times, there is no doubt but that he could become favourite to win a final. However, if he has only just managed to qualify in his heats, it's likely that his price will increase and that he will be a long shot outsider. This is what we had done with *Cherry Rocket* and here he was - a finalist in the Grand Prize. The distance of the race was 525 yards. The Enniscorthy track record for this distance stood at 29.90 seconds. By winning his two heats in times of 30.60 and

30.70, he had ensured that he would be a very long shot. The favourite for the night was most likely to be *Winsome Mary* with a time of 30.40.

The six dogs who qualified for the final on 23rd September 1959 were, in trap order: 1. *Winsome Mary,* 2. *Orla's Best,* 3. *Nimble Billy,* 4. *Kirsten's Pet,* 5. *Behewhohemay* and 6. *Cherry Rocket.*

The best traps to be drawn in were one and six because there was one trouble-free side on the inside and another on the outside. In the middle traps, a dog could be hindered or impeded by other dogs on both sides.

The dogs were put in the traps, the electric hare started its circuit of the track, the alarm for the public to be ready sounded and people scrambled to the stand to obtain a good view of the race. The judges were in position on the judging stand overlooking the finishing line - all was ready.

As the hare sped by the traps 'Cogs' Connors activated the lever, the traps sprang up, the greyhounds 'broke' and the race was on. *Kirsten's Pet* was a consistently good breaker and showed to the fore. *Orla's Best* and *Nimble Billy* jostled each other and both lost ground. Number one, *Winsome Mary,* was not a good breaker but showed early pace to the first bend. She was the favourite to win at 4/6 and would be the greyhound to beat. My money, however, was on *Cherry Rocket* at 7/1. Every penny I owned, all forty-seven pounds sterling of it, was laid down in an all or bust gamble on my uncle's greyhound.

He broke behind number four but was on the outside and did not have any trouble. *Kirsten's Pet* led the field at the first bend and was followed by number five, *Behewhohemay,* who had also had a good break.

The dogs passed the Powerhouse and *Orla's Best*

started making ground on the leaders as they raced down the far side. *Winsome Mary* took up the running at this stage and at the third bend she was ahead of the field, followed by *Nimble Billy* and *Cherry Rocket* who was also making ground and into whose staying power my financial prospects were entrusted.

As they came around the last bend into the straight headed for the finishing line, *Nimble Billy* and *Winsome Mary* collided; both lost ground and as a result were out of the rest of the race. *Behewhohemay* was now ahead of *Orla's Best, Cherry Rocket* and *Kirsten's Pet*. They were in the straight heading for home, forty yards to go and *Orla's Best* was finishing with a strong rally as she passed *Behewhohemay*, closely followed by *Cherry Rocket* and *Kirsten's Pet. Orla's Best* was now neck and neck with *Cherry Rocket* and *Kirsten's Pet* was a length away in third place. As they crossed the finishing line, it was impossible to tell who had won and the judge called for a photo finish. It would take a further seven or eight minutes to develop and print the final result.

At last the announcer's voice came over the public address: 'Result of photo finish: Winner number six, Second number two, Third number four. Time 29.90, equalling the Enniscorthy track record. Distances: A neck between first and second, a half-length between second and third. ' Our fortunes were made and the celebrations lasted for a week.

They were there when we moved in

Angela O'Connor

They were there when we moved in. The fish.
Gold. Some of them as big as a cod. Where they live is a big pond, with plants and crazy paving surrounding it.

The fish feed on pellets. They all come to the surface when it is feeding time.

They are not my favourite pets. Sometimes I think about doing something awful such as putting a few piranhas in the pond. A field day they'd have...

My friend keeps hers in a big tank in the kitchen. A very angry fish, white in colour with two rows of sharp teeth. I think it might have had pink or blue eyes. You could not touch the tank at all or he would become aggressive and go berserk. I thought he was really ugly and the tank was the best place for him.

I wouldn't want him in my living room at all.

Strawberries & Cream

Mary B. Keyes

Loganberries, blackcurrants and gooseberries grew in our back garden, just one bush of each so they were easy to pick and we used to make pots of jam from them. Strawberries and raspberries were grown by the local farmers and we had to travel to pick them, usually in groups. The farmer would collect us in his car and we would drive to the farm to begin the fruit-picking.

Early morning dew would be glistening on the grass in the Abbey field - a field I used to take a short cut through, on my way to Butlers' fruit farm. The strawberry plant would dry out in the morning sunshine. Those rays were very warm on our necks as we bent down to pick the berries and we would all complain of sore backs at the end of the day.

There was good communication between the pickers, conversation flowed easily. The farmer would raise his voice to get us to come and empty the buckets. He would pay us at the end of each day from a big wad of notes. He was usually in a good mood and happy with the day's work.

After the pick was over, we would take a shower and dress up and get ready to travel to the nearby market town where we could spend some of our hard-earned money. One year, I bought a new denim miniskirt in a boutique, to wear to the Strawberry Festival. This fair happened every year and it lasted one whole week. It was great fun. All the good-looking girls would get their partner-for-life during the festival - it was a stomping ground for many local marriages.

The Strawberry Queen was picked every year in Murphy Floods Hotel. Music by well-known bands and singers would be played on the Market Square. Strawberries and cream would be on sale for the duration of the festival although some people preferred to have theirs with champagne!

I picked fruit up to about Inter. Cert. It was my regular summer job and I never got fed up - even though sometimes I'd break out in hives. The smell of strawberries always reminds me of summer.

A Model's Diary

Mary B. Keyes

7.00 a.m.

I awoke to the sunlight shining through the window. It was going to be a very hot day. It was the 9th of June 2001, the day of the *Make & Model Fashion Show*. I jumped out of bed, pulled back the curtains and opened the window. I looked out at the village green where the marquee was erected. The workmen had arrived and had started putting together the catwalk and arranging the seats.

8.00 a.m.

I went to the bathroom and had a shower. I donned my towelling robe and went downstairs to the kitchen to prepare breakfast. I had two *Weetabix* with ten strawberries and Greek Natural Yoghurt. This was followed by a poached egg and two grilled rashers, a slice of wholemeal toast and some freshly brewed coffee. I also had a glass of pure still *Ballygowan* water.

10 a.m. to 12 p.m.

I had an appointment with the hairdresser and beautician to try different hairstyles and make-up. It went well and everyone was happy.

1.00 p.m.

I had a light lunch – a salad of lettuce, tomato, scallions, a boiled egg and a slice of cooked ham; accompanied by some brown bread and tea.

2.00 p.m. to 5 p.m.

I was busy meeting the rest of the contestants and around 3 p.m. we had a dress rehearsal and everything went fine. I was chosen to be the first to model on the catwalk. Nerve-wracking...

6.00 p.m.

Two hours to go! It was a mad rush. I had a shower, a visit from the hairdresser, the beautician and then I had to dress up. My outfit was a red top and a yellow and red plaid trousers along with a nice pair of heels.

8.00 p.m.

The time had arrived! I had butterflies in my tummy... We were all lined up. I was top of the line. My name was called. I climbed the steps to the ramp and had to walk halfway down, give a twirl and walk back up the catwalk to the top. Then a final twirl and back down the steps. When it was all over I felt elated and exhausted.

The Old Box in the Corner

Lillian McLoughlin

We have become a nation of Couch Potatoes. People have become less sociable; there is very little conversation, all because of T.V. If you speak now when telly is on, you are very quickly told to be quiet.

With modern technology, there is no time for fun and games among children nowadays. Our grandparents were more into music - they made their own entertainment and they were happy. Children are spoiled now and get bored easily. We should be taking more exercise and mixing with one another.

So get up us Couch Potatoes and Get Moving!

My Grandparents' Farm

Barry Mitten

There were two fields I used to work in as a teenager, on my grandparents' farm near Athenry, in Galway. In one field, there were ten or twelve whitehead bullocks grazing, eyes down. I wouldn't be frightened of them usually. You'd get odd moments when you were - but I could overcome the fear. I used to stand and wait and look, let the bullocks pass. And then go on to the next field.

I'd see dandelions first and buttercups in May, nettles and thistles scattered. You'd expect those fields to have long grass but they wouldn't, due to the bullocks grazing.

The vegetable field had two or three different varieties in drills: potatoes, swede turnip, cabbage and carrots. We used to pick them and hack the tops off the turnips and carrots. In the potato field, we'd shake the mud off. At about seven at night, my Granny Byrne would cook up a big feed of spuds. Spare ribs with fried potatoes. It tasted filling but savoury.

Walking across those two fields in Galway used to make me feel strong because I was able to do work. For the first time I could feel my own physical strength, which made me feel good.

Cavalier King Charles Spaniel

Philip Priestly

The Cavalier King Charles Spaniel is the largest breed in the Toy group. The colours are Blenheim, Ruby, Black and Tan and Tricolour. A Cavalier weighs twelve pounds and measures twelve to thirteen inches to the shoulder. Their expression gives an impression of a generous nature.

I own a Cavalier - his name is Sam. I got him from a breeder from Adamstown in 1995. He is the last of his litter but remarkably, has survived and is thriving. Sam is twelve years old and is a very active dog. He enjoys walks every day. He is well-mannered and doesn't snatch a biscuit from me when I offer it to him. When he first arrived, Sam slept in a kennel but didn't get accustomed to it. Now, he sleeps in the shed in a basket. Previously, he had a wicker basket but chewed it, so now it has been replaced by a plastic one.

Sam is an intelligent dog and very strong. He loves lying in the sun on warm days. He goes everywhere with me and is my loyal companion. Sam's coat is silky and smooth. He gets a bowl of food once a day. He has provided me with much enjoyment and laughter in all the time since I have had him. The Cavalier is a suitable dog for people who have small, confined spaces.

The Morgans of Cornwall

Philip Priestly

Cornwall in southwest England is a jagged peninsula, which claims it has a separate identity to the rest of the United Kingdom. The Duchy of Cornwall is bordered by Devon. Once famous for tin mining, which ended in 1997 in Castle Croftie, the Duchy is shrouded in myths and legends, say for example the story of the birthplace of King Arthur.

But in the numerous fishing villages of southwest Cornwall, they speak of a different creature that lurks in the rockpools and seaweed beds, for this is the home and realm of the Morgans. In appearance, they are handsome compared to dwarves, as they have long, regal necks. The men and women wear conch shells and have elegant, flowing clothing. Their dwellings are called cathedrals and are hewn under the rock. Their food is seacows, which provide them with meat and milk. Otherwise, they are vegetarian.

The Morgans are peaceful in nature and help those who were unfortunately shipwrecked on the treacherous Cornish coastline. They tend to those who are stranded. If you are walking on a sandy beach in Northern Brittany or along a shingle beach in Southern Cornwall, you just might catch sight of these little creatures running among the seaweed.

There is Light at the end of the Tunnel

Tony Allen

Today, I am in really good form.
I've not a care in the world.
I have money in my pocket and cigarettes.
The weather is great; I'm busy with the course
And so happy to be alive.

Not have I always been this way.
I suffer from an illness called Bipolar Disorder and
Manic Depression.
Manic Depression creeps up on me.
Very seldom do I realise this.
Sometimes when I get elated, I can't think straight.
Sometimes when I get depressed, I can't sleep or eat.
Sometimes I do irrational things.

I suffer from another disorder called Alcoholism.
I have hurt an awful lot of people on the way.
I am on the up and up at the moment through medication,
Helpful nurses, confidence and self-awareness.

I hope I will get better. I know I will.
I will pay back to everyone who has stood by me.
I will achieve the best I can.

Prayer

Tony Allen

I believe in God.
I believe in the Bible but I wasn't always this way.
I'm named Anthony after the saint: my mother and my
grandmother prayed for a baby boy - and here I am,
a baby no more.

I don't believe in the church.
I don't believe in mass but a bit of prayer always helps.
Whatever you are: Catholic, Protestant, Jewish, Buddhist,
Whatever your faith, that's your belief and you should be left
alone in your own privacy to pray.

My flat is my church
And nobody gives out or tells me when or where to say
my prayers.
So I pray all the time - whenever I get a quiet moment.

My Gentle Mother

Maureen O'Connor

I had a Mother who loved me so much.
And I loved her just as much.
She was gentle out, with a lovely smile.
Spoke her mind and was very loyal and true.
Maureen was her name also.

A black head of hair, short and dead straight.
Dark red lipstick with round earrings of gold.
Not a tall woman but big to me as a child.
Friendly, generous, liked to joke and laugh.
A graceful manner - not inclined to rush and race.
Outstanding.

I used help her at home: sweeping the kitchen floor,
Bringing in the milk in the morning.
Putting the bottles out at night.
Making up the beds - we worked alongside one another.
Side by side, she'd wash and I'd dry the delph.
Some days you'd smell the washing powder off her clothes.
But after she'd get a bath, the scent of Palmolive soap
took over.
That's the smell that brings her back to me.

She will always have a place in my heart.

A Tribute to the Family of Hayden

William Hayden

We are a large family of ten.
Very dedicated to our heritage.
Very dedicated to our families.
We have a habit for being honest in our
commitment to live a normal life.
A very nice family to get on with.

I will name the family of Haydens:
First is Andy, the oldest.
John, second.
Willie third and Martin fourth.
Marion fifth. Kevin sixth.
Gus seventh, Bridget eighth.
Cathy ninth, R.I.P.
Donal tenth.
A mighty family full of zest for life.

I, William, have the courage for writing this
letter with dignity and pride.

A Tribute to my sister Cathy, R.I.P.

William Hayden

I remember Cathy as a good girl.
Full of ambition.
Strong as a horse.
Reared two nice boys.
Honest as could be.
She was very fond of my Mother and Father.
I, William, had a lot of time for her.
As time went on she started to get weak, the poor old craythur.
Thought she was alone.
But she wasn't.
We were there with her.
Go raibh míle maith agat a Cathy.

Mary-Ellen

by E. Ryan

The vision I have of my Great Aunt Mary-Ellen was of a silent craythur.

Mary-Ellen, when walking, showed me how to be relaxed in motion. My Auntie sat in her favourite armchair. She would take from the cupboard a green comb, then she would let down her hair. Her nut-brown hair would fall down to waist length, straight as a die.

Mary-Ellen was not too serious. She had her own silent temperament. I never seen her laugh. The woman was a housekeeper for many a year.

This Great-Aunt of mine was married. Her husband used her. I believe he dragged the last penny from her. This man was too fond of the drink and Mary-Ellen had a few bob after selling her house. This Tipperary man drank every penny of Mary-Ellen's purse. She even had to buy cigarettes from the house money for him.

A Bright Darkness

by E. Ryan

Years ago, these places used to be called huckster's shops. They were a small supermarket. Even though there were windows and a main door, the atmosphere was dark. A bright darkness. Each shop had its own distinctive shade and odour. The odour comes from the amalgamation of different food scents.

Years ago, the products were all open to the air. Biscuits were packed in tins and the lovely scent of them could be smelled if the tins were not airtight. You might also sniff a bacon joint, hanging up on the S hooks.

As a ten year-old kid, I used to get summer holiday work off of *H.B. Ices* and help the salesman on the lorry. Before starting on the road to make a delivery to these huckster shops, every box of ice cream was checked by the office staff. When the day's work was done, the unsold products were listed and any remaining ice cream was deducted from the morning list.

When on the road, the driver would take one half-hour for lunch. A sandwich was in order. Some days a pack of biscuits. A delicacy would be a bottle of milk taken from the truck freezer. This was when the mobile transport had no freezer unit. Inside the truck was fitted out with aluminium and the milk was cooled by the frozen ice cream.

Walking into one of these shops to make a delivery, even the sawdust floor in there had its own special scent. A sawdust floor when damp has a lovely aroma. The nicest of these shops was the one with a tree covering the outside wall of the building.

The mood of those huckster shops is not to be found nowadays. The up-to-date shopkeepers have brightened up the darkness, so the whole atmosphere, the scent of the building has changed forever.

Pony Sale

Orla Slevin

By nature, Connemara ponies are gentle, calm and quiet. What appeals to me about these docile animals, is their relaxed temperament. My Dad had two of them, light grey in colour, about fifteen hands height, each soft mane neatly plaited with white elastics. They loved to be rubbed down along the nose.

A very important part of caring for a Connemara pony, after galloping him, is to walk him down the lane, unsaddle him and cool him down with running water. I often watched my nephew Mark doing this.

A couple of days before one of my Dad's animals was sold, a vet came to mark a paper with all the pony's details such as breeding, microchip, health and all the rest. As a special treat we gave him a rack of hay as well as nuts and oats mixed through together. These were all his favourites.

My sister-in-law Elizabeth brought him up out of the stable to load him into the horsebox. Liz drove him to Goresbridge, County Kilkenny, where the pony sales happen. To show the buyers what the ponies do, the sellers get a young jockey to jump the animals on the day.

One buyer was from Thomastown. He was interested after only ten minutes. This buyer noticed how well the pony was jumping. A good oul' lepper! The man from Thomastown had made up his mind: as soon as the auctioneer opened the bidding, the buyer would be ready...

The auctioneer was a tallish man whose hat was too big for him. It kept slipping down his forehead, annoying the hell out of him!

Well, the bidding was fast and furious. Finally, the Thomastown buyer's bid was accepted. There and then, a cheque was handed over and my Dad's placid pony was taken away. Liz watched for the last time as his hooves clattered up into the horsebox. She smiled happily as the grey lepper was driven off.

The Tinahely Show

Orla Slevin

The first thing I would go to when I visit the County Show in Tinahely, is the Poultry Tent. All around the sides are ducks, hens, all different pure-bred breeds such as Brahma, Cuckoo Marin, Khaki Campbell. I like the great variety of colours.

Next I go for a wander around the stalls. I always head for the cheese stands and I taste all sorts of cheeses such as Blue, Brie and Wexford Cheddar.

Pets Corner is very popular with the chaps. Here, you'll find all sorts of rabbits, cats, hamsters, tortoises, guinea pigs and birds. I remember once I saw a lop-eared rabbit. I thought he was cute and would have liked to take him home. He was a foot long with a soft, grey coat.

My next stop was usually the stock field where the farm animals were judged. You would see different types of cows here: Friesian, Charolais and Herefords. Aberdeen Angus is my favourite because of their striking colour.

Jacob sheep are unusual because of their brown coat, like light chocolate. The reason I go and see the pigs is because they are endearing. They have hard skin and are pink in colour.

My last stop is always at the Dog Show. The owners walk their dogs around the ring while the judges pick which animal is the best. My personal favourite is the Shih Tzu because I love their funny face!

The Dunbrody

Noel Galavan

It began on the dry dock, in New Ross, on the Waterford side,
Over where the old barge factory was.
About thirty of us on the boat-building team, making a brand new *Dunbrody*.
There was a good, friendly atmosphere. Great craic.
We'd a right time cracking jokes and having a laugh.
Most of the men were from town, so I knew a lot of them already.
We started from scratch, building a replica of the original ship.
Building a boat from nothing.
My job was to cut timber: big, long planks.
I was cutting the lengths of wood from eight in the morning up until five.
Better than sitting around doing nothing.
I hated that, I'd get bored.
But it's a cold spot over there, with the wind coming in off the river.
We were all working out in the open air, no shelter.
If it rained, the timber got wet, same as ourselves!

Thinning Beet

John Kehoe

I remember thinning the beet for farmers when I got my holidays from school during my teenage years - a long time ago now! In those days, we took great pride and interest in our work. We would haggle with the farmers over how much or what price a drill of beet was paid at. Usually the price would be around sixpence - that's six old pennies.

Thinning beet could be a hard task at times. You wore kneecaps. They would be a bag tied on your legs above and below the knee. We were usually paid by the drill and we'd tell the farmer how many drills we had done when we were finishing up. Often, we'd feed ourselves with a flask or bottle of tea, along with some white pan loaf or brown bread.

You would space the beet about six inches apart and pull all the weeds in between. There was no precision sowing that time! Your hands would blister at first but after a while, they would be alright. When you'd start work in the morning, it was great listening to all the birds singing and maybe watching some rabbits out grazing first thing.

My First Day at School

John Kehoe

I remember my first day at school very well.
I can recall my mother telling me I had to start national school. It was she who held my hand and brought me in.
That was alright.
So I started my very first day.
I remember feeling it was a strange place to be.
Especially the nuns with their black and white uniforms...
I was turned off with it straight away.
So at lunchtime, I climbed over the school wall and ran off up the road.
But I was spotted!
Two of the older boys ran after me and escorted me back to school.

Hurling

Michael Kinsella

I like going to Croke Park.

I love the hurling very well.
I do have a good time on the bus.

I went to all the games the time we won the All-Ireland.
Martin Storey used to be playing in all the matches.

Even the weather was usually very good.
After, I would get chips and fish.

I used to go to Wexford Park to see the hurling.

Handball

Michael Kinsella

I was taught to play handball by my third cousin, Martin, when I was about fifteen or sixteen years of age. Martin said you need to be fast and have a hard hand.

Sometimes the lads would all go off without me. To play handball. But Martin was a great man for the chaps. He'd say 'Come on, I'll bring you.'

We'd go driving up the road in Martin's Toyota Hiace van, a lovely yoke. You'd be high up over the hedges and could see out over the road for miles in front of you.

He'd bring me up for a feed after playing and to see them all at home. There'd be Johnny and Mary and Martin and me. Sarah, their daughter, used have a great welcome for me. I wouldn't miss a week. They'd meet me at the door and invite me in. Big smiles all round.

I'd sit down by the coal fire and Martin would talk away. I'd sit by him at the table and Mary'd feed me and hand me a cup of tae. Getting a feed was great - a right tae. White bread and butter and jam. Currant cake. I never went without tae in that house.

Mary and Johnny and Martin are all gone now.

Fruit Picking in Co. Wexford

William Doyle

When I was a little boy, I used to go picking fruit in the townsland of Coolbarrow. There were sceachs and bushes all over the country roads. Wild brambles stretching up seven foot high. The prevalent fruits were blackberries.

In my hand, I held a little blue bucket. I picked blackberries off the sides of ditches; stretching and pulling, reaching and bending.

After an hour or so, my plastic bucket was half-full so I would take a rest, sitting down among the foliage of the ditch - so long as there were no thorns! As far as the eye could see, there were blackberries all over the intermeshing briars.

When I was finished picking for the day, I got home in about five minutes and handed my mother my hoard. The berries were luscious, shiny and glossy. They were plump and filled with sweet juice. Mam used to make them into beautiful blackberry jam that tasted fruity and gorgeously sweet! Its colour was rich and sheeny.

Coffee Drinking Rituals in Agios Nicolaos

William Doyle

I like the taste of the ground coffee that my mother
keeps in a jar.
South American Java and coffee beans from Brazil.
I take a sip and though I am sitting in Ireland,
I can remember the strong taste of the coffee we had,
my brother and I,
In Agios Nicolaos, on Crete.
The bright blue sea was before us,
Rays of sunshine warming the water,
And cricket sounds coming from the countryside.
We were served breakfast in a ritualistic style:
Crispbread and marmalade.
Strong coffee and sugar and milk.
The long-necked coffee pot was made out of white porcelain.
When poured, our drink had a harsh aroma.
A heavy smell.
Dark, percolated, nearly black.
Undissolved granules in a liquid,
Swirling somewhere between brown and black.
The taste makes you feel fulfilled and full of caffeine.
It rises you and rouses you.

Foal

John Yates

I had experience of mares foaling, with an Irish draught mare that I bought with an elderly friend of mine at Goresbridge sales. She was a beautiful grey mare with very good bone and good confirmation. She had three foals for me and I had delivered them on my own. But I had moved in with my friend Stella and her mare, *Fairy River,* was expecting.

We stayed up many nights watching her on a small television, which was connected from the stable to the house by a cable. She was a chestnut mare and had won four point-to-point races. Therefore, we hoped her foal would be valuable, all the more if it was a colt.

The mare would lie down and force a bit, but then stand up and be alright. Then at other times, she would walk purposefully around the stable in a circle, making a pathway in the good straw that was on the stable floor.

But late one night at about one o'clock in the morning, a change came upon the mare. She walked harder and soon we realised that she was beginning to sweat. We knew that the arrival of the foal was imminent. This was confirmed when she put out the blob which is the water sack. She was lying down and getting up and properly in labour, heaving and forcing and making a good deal of noise.

Then she lay with her bottom about five feet from the wall. The foal was beginning to come. It arrives with the two front legs first, followed by the head. I swore I saw the head move.

But suddenly there was trouble. The foal seemed to be almost stuck. Stella and I grabbed a leg each and started to pull. It was very difficult as the foal was so tight in the mare that we could only pull our hardest as the mare herself forced. She was helping us and we were helping her.

By inches we pulled the foal out but it was taking too long and the foal was lifeless. We were very upset especially myself as this was my first foaling for Stella and it had gone wrong. It was heartrending to see the dead foal lying on the straw... However, we had saved the mare who could easily have died too. She got up although she was also distressed to see her foal dead. We took the dead body outside and soon after the mare passed the afterbirth.

But it was not until the following day that we found out that we had been lucky. A very experienced man came and noticed that the foal's belly was too large and also that the placenta was a bad colour. He said that the foal was already dead in the mare before it was born. I said that I had seen the foal's head move but he stated that it was just the pressure on the head that gave the appearance of movement.

The sequel to this is that *Fairy River* had a good healthy foal the following year and the next seven foals Stella and I had were all colts.

Hallowe'en

William Colfer

I was at home with my father near Foulksmills one Hallowe'en. A boy was going around about eight o'clock at night. A young boy of twelve or thirteen. I never found out who he was. Never, even to this day.

It was a fine night, dry and all, bright enough, not much wind. I don't know whether I knew it was Hallowe'en or not, I hadn't much interest in it that time. 'Twas for children - they like getting the money. Neighbours' children. Three or four of 'em. Carrying on. Dancing. Not singing but clowning for a few bob, a few shillings.

They were happy. Children are like that, ain't they? They loves to get a bit of money. If I had money in me pocket, I'd throw it out on the ground. I'd like to see them all diving for it. Whoever got it would keep it. Tenpenny bits.

This boy knocked at the door anyway and I answered. When I first heard the knock I didn't know what it was. My father was a mechanic so people'd often come looking for him at all hours. Farmers especially.

This boy was wearing a fawn-coloured coat. Asking. Pleading. 'E'er a few pennies for a poor boy?'

I stepped outside then and he started talking. About four foot ten or five foot. Thin but healthy for his age. He'd a mask on and was all covered up. It was a white mask, made of cardboard.

This boy was messing about, talking and saying funny things. I tried to find out who he was but I couldn't. A mystery.

Don't know where he came from or who he was. His father might have been drinking in the pub.

He just walked away after, back along towards the pub. I went in to my father after a while. I didn't tell him much. I sat back down by the fire. My father used light it every evening: an electric fire for daytime and a coal one at night, lit with firelighters. Just the two of us and the flames...

Dehorning Cattle

William Colfer

About two weeks ago from today - March 25th 2008 - I went home for the day from a hostel belonging to St. Senan's hospital. On the way home, my brother Larry said he might be dehorning some cattle. When we arrived, we got the dinner and then he said he had twenty calves to take the horns off.

After the dinner, we went up to the sheds. We had to take the calves away from their mothers. A gate separated them and the cows were bawling after the calves who were less than three months old. We got them into the pen and put them, three or four at a time, into the crush. My brother had an electric machine for taking the horns off cattle. I had to grab hold of the calves and he would dehorn them.

Their little stumps were white in colour, only about an inch long. Larry'd press the machine down on the horns of each calf. There was a buzzing from the dehorning machine but the calves would be quiet while this was going on. It only lasted for a few seconds and it didn't cause them any pain. Smoke comes out of the stumps and there's a kind of acidy smell off it.

The calves were wild enough and you had to be right with them; if you weren't careful enough, they could walk on your feet or jump out over the gate.

I enjoy helping my brother Larry on the farm. My father is dead, and my mother, so I only have brothers and sisters, nephews and nieces now.

I grew up in the country and it's great to be back out

in the fresh air. When I came home from working in London, my uncle Martin asked me 'Would you see any cows around London?' Sure you'd never see anything like that over there and I surely missed the countryside.

Shaving

Martin Freeman

There's a lot to a man's beard. It depends on the growth you see. A man shaves in different ways. All the different moods are reflected in facial hairstyles.

He wears a moustache for going to the financial meetings - it gives him that air of superiority, that aura of responsibility, that he has an opinion too. It all borders on respectability. Take the goatee beard - it's for going to a Water Services meeting. This man will develop an opinion along with the beard.

Then there's the long sideburns for music or singing talent. The man sporting this style of facial hair, he'd usually be in his prime and be after reading an awful lot of books on modern development. He'd be a voice in the wilderness, an authority on different motivations - a great aura of quality about him, his ears sheltered by the two sideburns.

Now take the man who keeps his hair cut short, he likes to solve problems. His people might be in the army and he thinks it's right to keep his hair and beard trimmed. Often, he'll take his wife and kids to a party or to school functions. He likes to be tidy and to keep things at his fingertips. The priests and the patriarchs would be the same. When he sets the razor back down, later, he'll have to join the group of old men who are still at loggerheads with the world, arguing with one another. They have big bushy beards - it's all down to the hairdressing.

Shaving is like any part of nature. When you have your

work done, and done well, you'll be pleased with it. Yet you have hairdressers going round today and they just don't care. Their customers have to take their place on the bench and there they take their chances.

Cowboys

Paddy Galvin

I first saw one on television when I was only a chap. *The Virginian* was his name. Killing lads he was.

A cowboy has a hat on, a wide one and he goes around singing. He wears it when he's riding the horses the way he wouldn't get wet in the rain.

He wears a red shirt and blue cowboy trousers - like jeans but with leather bits over the top. He likes a black belt made out of snakeskin...

What impressed me was the way they used to live in cowboy houses made of timber, with bunk beds. Some would carry shotguns - if anyone'd attack them they'd use their weapons. See they'd carry smaller guns in their pockets and if someone wanted to kill them, they'd save themselves by going for this little gun.

We admired the way they were brought up to be able to ride a horse - sometimes with a saddle but more times without. Their job was to round up cattle, drive them across the desert. About four or five hundred head of cattle going across to the ranch in a great cloud of dust and dirt...

They'd make coffee on the fire and eat a meat sandwich. If they were livin' out, they'd have a canvas tent along with them for shelter. They'd lie down and go asleep under the stars. No one around to hear them snoring!

If I was a cowboy, I'd love riding a horse most. I learnt meself at home one time, begod I did. I said to the father "Are you going out to bring in the cows?" Next thing, I was gone missing - I was away off on the horse, only a rope around his neck. Now this horse never stirred, 'twas only me father usually rode him. But this time I was at the gate and the dog was gone up the fields after the cows. Riding a horse is not scary: I was up a little bit high but it felt grand. No bother.

Me father didn't say anything. Me mother came out and she took a photograph. She started smiling.

In the daytime cowboys look up at the sun - boiling, scorching and very warm. At night time, when it was dark, the moon'd be out, an' thousands of little stars, twinkling.

The desert would be lonely if you're on your own. 'Twouldn't be so bad if you had somebody with you, a person to talk to. But if you hadn't, you'd need someone to speak to and they wouldn't be there.

You'd have noplace to go only the quiet desert: no noise, no nothing. No move around at all. Silence. Nothing there only yourself. Quiet as could be. You'd feel sad then.

It's not an easy life, not when you're living on your own. Washing your own clothes in a basin or something, like people did years ago. And hang them out on a tree then to dry. And the sun'd be there in the middle of the day. And the poor cowboy sitting over in the shade, having a drink of water because he'd be dry. Sparing every mouthful. Taking his time drinking it. He'd be keeping some for a cup of tea later on.

Oh the cowboy passes his days wishing for fine weather. Worrying about wolves. Waiting for someone to attack him in his sleep. Longing for a wash in cold, clean water – next thing he's thinking about a dip in the lake, to cool himself off.

Now his arms and legs are moving out in the clear water. And a few Indian lads are creeping through the fields, watching the cowboy floating...

Journeys

The Journey Home

Moira Naessens

I like travelling and especially up to Gorey. I take *Bus Éireann* at the Gate Lodge at St. Senan's: the bus is at a quarter to eleven and, usually, Willie Roche waits there with me for the bus up to Gorey.

Once on our way, we pass the cemetery and also the bright display of red flowers. At the turn off, on the left outside Enniscorthy, is the garage that has brand new cars for sale.

As we are travelling the Dublin road on the bus, we are coming to Scarawalsh bridge. Sometimes during the year there would be bad floods at the little house; it could be flooded out from the river Slaney.

Coming just into Ferns, we are passing the famous Moynihan Brothers shop. They sell drums, guitars, pianos and so on. They are a famous band around Wexford and they perform for weddings and dances. Then, as we stop in Ferns, the bus driver lets the new passengers on. Bolger Brothers is on the right hand side going down, and also there is a Protestant Church. And then, we are off again on our homeward journey.

Eventually we arrive in Camolin. There are schoolchildren playing in the playground. Practical people are doing their shopping in the supermarket and butchers shops.

The new roundabout is just outside Gorey and in no length, we have finished our journey. The hospital is at the top of the town, with the statue of the Blessed Virgin, the Garda Station, and McCormick Brothers, the hardware shop. From one end of the street to further down, are all the various stores:

loads of people browsing and buying clothes and getting their morning shopping.

We stop at Whitmore's, the jewellery shop and then I get off and so does Willie Roche. He waits for his Mum to bring him back to Hollyfort. I head off down the Avenue and go home. At the end of our road is the big Dunnes Stores. I like to go shopping there for my Mum. Seeing the new Dunnes is exciting 'cos I know I'm at the end of my journey.

Jack Claeys, Con Artist

Gerald Morrin

Dan O'Callaghan, building contractor, perused the used machinery columns of a national magazine, *Irish Construction Review*, in search of a bargain. One can imagine his delight when he found an advertisement for a J.C.B. digger, two years old, offered by a vendor in Newry and going for €44,000.

This was a 2004 model and it sold for €63,000 when new, so Dan thought it would be ideal, as the price suited his pocket, and the digger itself should have more than ten years service to give to its operator.

He decided to ring the telephone number given immediately, in case somebody else might get it before him. A man, who gave his name as Jack Claeys, answered the call. According to Jack, the J.C.B. was on display in a machinery yard on Violet Hill in Newry. He said that it had been working the previous week and confirmed it to be in p.m.o. (perfect mechanical order); his firm were getting rid of it because there had been a downturn in their business. Dan said that €44,000 was a bit steep whereupon Claeys said he was empowered to reduce the price to €40,000 if he got paid in cash, but that was the only adjustment he could make.

When Dan told him that he was from Wexford, Jack replied that he could bring the J.C.B. south of the border and park it in the parking lot of *The Grill and Griddle* restaurant, near Dundalk, off the main Dublin-Belfast highway.

Claeys then asked Dan could he meet him for lunch in *The Grill and Griddle*. "Thursday April 4th, one p.m. at table number ten," was the rejoinder from Dan, for he was familiar with the restaurant. This was Friday March 29th, so he had time to make such arrangements as were necessary to withdraw the money from his bank; he also had to ring the management of the restaurant to reserve table number ten.

Dan was unwilling to buy a pig in a poke so he decided he would inspect the J.C.B. when Jack brought it south on the 4th. If he was satisfied, he would pay Jack in cash and take delivery of the machine in the parking lot. With their plans completed thus, and rendezvous settled, they bade each other "Goodbye".

Dan O'Callaghan collected the money from his bank on Wednesday 3rd April at 3 p.m. He put it in his attaché case, eighty notes of €500 each. The attaché case rested in Dan's safe on Wednesday night. On Thursday morning he personally re-checked the eighty notes and they were all there. He had left nothing to chance. He put the attaché case in a hidden compartment which was located under the driver's seat of the jeep in which he and his foreman would be travelling. He wanted to be on the road by 9.30 a.m. He filled the fuel tank of the jeep at 9 a.m., checked the tyres, oil and battery and was all set to go when his foreman arrived at 9.20 a.m.

Bill Williamson, the foreman, had worked with Dan for twenty-four years. It would be his job to drive the J.C.B. home safely to Wexford, before dark, if at all possible. They set out with no further delay and were passing through Ferrycarrig, just outside Wexford, at 9.30 a.m. They were in good time and expected to reach their destination at 12.45 p.m. or thereabouts. It was a fine spring day and driving conditions were excellent. The journey north was uneventful; Dan did all the driving and he did not stop until he pulled in to the parking lot of *The Grill and Griddle* restaurant at precisely 12.50 p.m.

Dan had made up his mind to leave the money in the jeep, while they were getting their meal, as he did not like the idea of bringing it into the restaurant. Having checked that the attaché case was still under the driver's seat, he locked the jeep – the two front doors and the door at the rear, and made certain that all the windows were closed and secured. All seemed safe and sound so Dan and Bill made their way towards *The Grill and Griddle.*

There was no J.C.B. digger to be seen as they walked through the parking area; this did not alarm Dan as he knew that Jack Claeys could be delayed along the way for many reasons - heavy traffic, breakdown, puncture, accident and so on. It was 12.57 p.m. when the Manager of the restaurant showed them to table number ten which had been reserved for three.

They sat down and without hesitation Dan asked for the menu. Neither of them would have a drink but both were hungry; as Dan wanted Bill on the road for home by 2.30 p.m., he was not going to stand on ceremony and did not wait for Jack Claeys arrival but ordered for Bill and himself almost immediately. Their soup was served at 1.10 p.m. and the main course arrived at 1.20 p.m. Dan was getting uneasy. At 1.40 p.m., with no news of Jack Claeys, Dan got up from his unfinished meal and told Bill he was going to ring Claeys' number.

His diary, wherein he had noted the number, was tucked away in the inside pocket of his topcoat, which was outside in the back of the jeep. He made his way to where he had parked.

As far as he could see, there were no J.C.B. diggers

at all in the parking area. Approaching the jeep, Dan thought there was something wrong and then he saw it - the window of the driver's door was broken. He could not believe it at first and for a few seconds he was at a complete loss and did not know where to turn. He fumbled for the keys and got the door open. He tilted the driver's seat forward, exposing the lid of the hitherto concealed compartment; he lifted the lid and his worst fears were confirmed - the attaché case was gone.

There was no use crying over spilt milk. Broken glass lay scattered on the floor of the jeep and outside on the tarmac. He decided that he would not report his loss to the Gardaí as he realised how foolish he had been and that it was likely he was 'set up' for the episode anyway. He felt he had better tell Bill, so he locked the driver's door and returned to the restaurant.

Bill was just finishing his coffee when Dan told him that the purchase money had been stolen. Bill immediately said that Dan should report the matter to the Gardaí but Dan would have none of it. They sent for the Manager whose name was Silas MacAfee, and asked him if anything suspicious had been seen or reported. He replied that he had not seen or heard anything. "Is there C.C.T.V. in the parking lot?" asked Dan. Silas said there was but that it was out of order at the moment. Dan could not help thinking how convenient that was for the thieves.

Nothing could be done to recover the money and Dan was adamant that he would not contact the Gardaí. He would pay for the meal and they would make their way home. Bill drove the jeep to Wexford as Dan was still in a state of shock - his mind was racing, his hands were shaking and he found it difficult to concentrate.

This story should have concluded here with a happy ending, but, as fact is stranger than fiction, (the story is based on an actual occurrence) it does not do so. Moreover, the money was never recovered, the crime was never reported or investigated and the thieves escaped with their loot scot-free. Had Dan O'Callaghan been content to pay all his bills by cheque or had he reported the crime to the authorities, it might have been a different story. As it was, he had to be content to get up out of his bed on the 5th of April, a wiser, but a far poorer man.

A Summer Vacation

Mary B. Keyes

The day had dawned. It was time to get ready to go to the airport for our journey to Istanbul in Turkey where the east meets the west. Istanbul straddles the Bosphorous Strait: with a skyline studded with domes and minarets, it is one of the world's great romantic cities.

I stepped off the ferryboat that brought us from the train to our hotel and into the hub of Istanbul, the Bazaar. I was amazed at the colours of the different races in their ethnic clothes. The Bazaar was full of exotic carpets, all different shades: golden yellows, blood reds and snow whites. There was brass, silverware, the sharp smell of spices and the noisy haggling with the stall owners drowning out all sound. Only the Turkish music could barely be heard.

Mid-week, on Wednesday, we decided to pay a visit to Topkapi Palace, home to the sultans until the nineteenth century. We were in luck: the International Music Festival was on. Mozart's opera The *Abduction from the Seraglio,* which is performed in the palace every summer, was being staged. We enjoyed it very much because it was both soothing and lively.

For the next few days, we went to the beach to get a tan. The weather was lovely, it was very sunny and hot so we all got as brown as berries. In the mornings, I did some shopping for souvenirs to take home: Turkish delight, traditional dolls and carved wooden pipes. On Sunday, we left for Ireland, tired but refreshed after our summer holiday.

On the Move

Michael Carroll

My journey begins in St. Enda's, on the first floor of the hospital.

Starting out, it seems like a daunting journey. Leaving the ward, I continue walking until I get to the new lift - now more spacious than what it used to be in the past. The old lift was very noisy but this one isn't.

I press a button that says zero and when the doors open again, I'm on the ground floor looking out at the side of a drinks machine. Straight ahead I am faced with a blank wall.

I head for the entrance hall, leading me to the front door. Once outside, I catch the handles of the silver railings for support and make my way down the steps.

Next, I go across a field of grass, passing the rusty seesaw and swings. Very occasionally, children do use them. Today they stand silent and still.

Crossing the grass, coming towards *Skillbase*, I walk up a long, leafy laneway. When I reach the gravel and hear my feet crunching stones, that's when I know I've arrived.

Now, my form is relaxed, my first journey of the day is done. I won't be on the move again until lunchtime.

Weekend Away

Kirsten Sellhorn

In 1979 and 1980, I went to the Anti-Nuclear demonstrations which took place in Carnsore Point. I went along with my brothers and some cousins who had come to Ireland on holidays.

These demonstrations were on in the summer and were quite big - a large crowd gathered, music was played, meetings took place and many easy-going people mixed and mingled. There were groups of Hare Krishnas as well who had an area all to themselves and they gave out food which was vegetarian and even egg-free. They sold items and artefacts to do with their religion and got people to chant with them. The main belief of the Hare Krishnas, I think, was that human beings and living creatures have spirits and so they believed in a type of reincarnation and their god was Krishna.

I connect the whole Hare Krishna thing with colour and they certainly seemed to give out an aura of happiness. The men had their hair shaved with just a bit left in a type of ponytail. Their clothes were like saris in orange and yellow and these were even wrapped around their babies. They wore sandals made of materials other than leather and the women wore colourful white saris with blue patterns.

My friends and I enjoyed Carnsore Point and whatever way it turned out, nuclear power didn't come about in Ireland. It was to be another few years 'til I was to run into Hare Krishnas again. There was a married couple from Wexford who I got to know, and when I was working in Wexford town in a hotel, I found out they used to do meals - Indian or Hare Krishna style. They had these meals at their home and it was up to oneself what one paid. I used to go now and again.

I kept in touch with Margaret and Stephen and then, in 1984, they suggested I spend a weekend with a group who had a house very near Dublin. The weekend they decided for me was quite eventful: a restaurant was being opened which was going to be run by Hare Krishnas and the head of the group was due to be staying.

I went up on the bus to *Bus Áras* in Dublin that first evening and I got a taxi to the house. Margaret and Stephen were there to meet me and they took me to their apartment. The whole house was divided into apartments for the different couples and individuals. I had trousers on and they actually asked me to change into a skirt or dress! I was also asked not to smoke which I thought was a little bit negative.

We had herbal tea and biscuits with some other members of the household and at eight o'clock it was time for bed because we would have to get up at four in the morning. This seemed a bit outlandish but I think that monks from other religions do the same. I couldn't sleep straight away because it was too early and I felt a bit keyed up about the weekend. Also, I missed my cigarettes.

I was woken at four and it was a little bit bright because it was summer. The first thing we had to do was have a cold shower. This was a custom of the religion, a kind of penance. Then we chanted Hare Krishna prayers with beads, walking around a garden. At five, we had breakfast of cereal with milk and honey, followed by wholemeal biscuits and bread. The men ate separately from the women.

Later on that morning, a few women and myself

organised a car for us to go into Dublin. We were to give out leaflets about the new restaurant. It was all very cheerful as we headed for the city centre and we spent the whole day there, handing out leaflets near Grafton Street.

That evening we had more delicious vegetarian dishes which the Hare Krishna people make so well and then I was asked to help make food for the celebration meal with the leader and a guru who was coming. That evening, they arrived and there was singing and chanting, followed by the feast. One thing I was against was that us women had to sit and squat in the hallway while the Hare Krishna monks had a nice dining room. That sort of decided me that I had had enough. So when the festivities were over, I told Margaret I was heading back to Wexford. I made the excuse that I was a bit fluey...

The next morning, I made my way back to a bus stop after saying my goodbyes. The people were so hospitable to me, it wasn't their fault that it didn't work out and overall, the visit was quite an enjoyable experience.

The bus stop was near a newsagents and I bought a paper, a fattening bar of chocolate and a nice romantic novel. I made myself comfortable and read for a while. The bus came after a bit and once again I was headed back on the road for Wexford.

My Love of Wexford

Tony Allen

My earliest holiday memories are from Wexford. My mother, my father, my sister, brother and myself, used to come to Wexford for two weeks in July. We used to go down to a caravan and my father always brought his accordion. He played in pubs in the evenings. We made great friends and were down visiting the same friends, each and every year.

As a teenager, my pals and I rented holiday homes at Courtown near Gorey. When I met my wife and we had our eldest son, Daniel, we used to spend time in various holiday places. We continued to try out different resorts like Kilmore Quay, Ballygarrett, Rosslare Strand and Rosslare Harbour. As my job started to get more stressful, we used to come down more often.

When my fourth child, Ryan, was born, we bought a caravan and put it on a site down in Carne and we came down from Friday evenings. My wife, Deirdre, would go to the different pubs and sing in them, with the children. I would travel down on Friday and return on Monday morning.

As we got to love the place, we bought a house in Broadway, down by Our Lady's Island, about seven or eight years ago. My daughter Kimberly arrived and my youngest son Jack. He is a born Wexford man! All my children are or have attended school here.

We love Wexford and would only go back to Dublin on holidays...

Getting Out for a Break

Andy Donohoe

Looking forward to going home
And getting two nice thin cuts of bread and a small mug
of medium warm tea.

Looking out the taxi window,
You might see a few sheep in a field grazing turnips.
And you would see the deep river Slaney.
You would know it has taken in rainfall.
It's a sad part of the road.

Arriving home,
You would like to protect poor Mam. A passionate woman.

Watching television in Kilmyshall,
Hoping to be like the birds.
They can fly off and enjoy themselves someplace else...

Collaborations

Down Wexford Way

by Andy Donohoe & Larry Connick

Down Wexford way, there is a big sailing ship.
Burning hard coal.
With black smoke instead of white, coming out the chimney of the engine.
Underneath the boat, rakes of sharks come across salmon,
Just off Kilmore Quay Harbour.
The sharks are hungry - they swally up the salmon.
And then they turn direction.
They more or less find their way to the river Slaney in Bunclody and they sneak on down.
You wouldn't get to see them.
Then they'd rise their heads along by the furniture factory.
And they'd eat the white trout.
And they'd swim up so far, the craythurs,
They'd end up around Courtown Harbour.

Sunseekers

by Moira Naessens & William Doyle

Irish sun worshippers lazily lift their hands,
Daubing factor thirty over freckled arms.
Heads covered with straw sun hats.
Feet strapped into sandals, blister, burn and bake...

At the beach, radios blasting, blaring out the match.
Towels and togs thrown onto the sand,
Hot heads stuck into books.

Ripe bananas, currany scones, sandy salad sandwiches.
Fizzy minerals, hot coffee from a flask.
The picnic disappears in five minutes flat!
And then the pleading starts:
'Oh Mammy, can I've an ice-cream cone?'
'You'll do without. Wait 'til you go home!'
'Ah Mam, go on, get us a 99!'
'Alright, alright - ye're unnatural today!'

Away down where the water breaks,
A brave soul sticks in his toe.
He gasps! He jumps! He inches along.
Finally lets himself flop into the water,
Frightening crabs and jellyfish.

Towards sunset, these dazed worshippers
Pack up their belongings.
Seagulls scavenge, the tide laps out.
Crisp bags filled with sand lie abandoned on the beach...

Winter

by The Pink Group

Ice on the road.
Bare trees.
A green Christmas tree in a hot house.
Beautiful decorations in the hallway.
A coal fire smoking...

Hugo Neill

by Christy Doyle & Larry Connick

Hugo Neill, age forty. Prison Officer, Wexford Gaol, 1798.

I'm a fairly tall fella, six foot easy. Blocky build, clean-shaven, short brown hair kept neat. Brown leather shoes and a black, shiny uniform. I carry keys - a bunch of 'em. They make a rattling sound.

I love my job. Like going into work each morning. Enjoy giving orders. Bossing people around. Start work at seven in the morning. The first job is to give out the breakfast: watery whitish porridge. Cold as a stone. Next I goes to the medicine cabinet, gets any tablets the prisoners need for sore throats. And bandages for open wounds...

I write up a report sheet on the men: write on the way things would be. I'd be looking for marks to see if anyone was beaten up, looking for signs of rats - the doors chewed. Or everyday things, like we might need new woollen blankets.

What if a prisoner escaped or went missing? Oh then I'd have to write a report to the real bossman. A search party'd be organised. The missing man might hide down in the cellar, in among bits and pieces of furniture. I 'd have to push back any prisoner who tried to escape from his cell. I'd have to warn him 'Don't you ever do it again!' I might have to use the baton if there was a break out, causing terrible bruising and injury.

Once a day only, the men could go to the yard for exercise, walking endlessly. Once a month only, the local priest would be let in to visit.

It's possible that I could have ended up guarding a

neighbour or friend or even a relation. One day, I opened up a cell door only to find a young neighbour before me. Mattie Redmond. He was a bootlegger, caught for making beet wine during the rebellion. But he was captured and thrown into prison for a year.

Well he didn't feel too good inside there: sad, downhearted and lonely. I got a fright when I seen him. I wouldn't be tempted to let him go because I couldn't take pity on him above all the rest of the prisoners. Anyhow I'd lose my job and could even end up in prison myself. So I handed him his breakfast and shut the door again, trying not to hear the young man's voice calling out sorrowfully after me...

Seaside Scenes

by Noel Galavan, Michael Carroll and Kieran Sinnott

Sharks are swimming around the sea.
They are eating other fish.
People catch crabs and shrimps with their fishing nets.

Standing on Curracloe beach you might see:
Happy people splashing.
Pink crabs lurking, waiting for a shrimp.
Three beautiful young ones, strolling barefoot and paddling.

A Good Afternoon in Town

by Paddy Galvin, Larry Connick, Andy Donohoe
and Michael Kinsella

Doing a bit of shopping, see what's in the shops.
Buy a stripy red shirt - a summer one or a t-shirt.
Move on to the butcher's to buy a lamb chop - hard
to get a good one.
Then you'd have to get the spuds. They have to be got.
Golden Wonders - floury and buttery.
Cabbage. Carrots. Onions. Decent bit of coleslaw.
If you weren't able to get the coleslaw, give the lad
a good hiding!
The grandest dinner.
Couldn't be bothered with dessert - it's too tormentful.
Unless... Maybe ice cream.. or a dish of trifle. Or both!
A tumbler of Coke with the dinner.
Chance a glass of wine maybe?
Go for a walk then. Sit down on a seat out of the sun.
A drink in your hand, of ale or stout. Enjoying the fine day.
No one beside you, tormenting you.
You're on your own. No one annoying you.
Watching people crossing the road.
Cars going by, lorries, buses.
Walking back home, see flowers in the ditch.
Pick a few daffodils and bring them home with you.
Put them in a vase, up near the window.
They'd remind you that you were after being out.

Notes on Contributors

Andy Donohoe played a good bit of handball in his day.

Angela O'Connor was born and reared in London. On April 1st 1994 her family and herself moved to Wexford. It was snowing and blizzards on that day.

Barry Mitten is interested in the farm he was brought up on by his grandparents in Galway. He liked childhood in *'the West awake'*.

Bridget Murphy
In June, Bridget had the trip of a lifetime to Lourdes.

Christy Doyle lives in Gorey. He is a big fan of motorbikes and enjoys cooking Chicken Curry.

Claire Tuomey is a freethinking frivolous fun seeker. Presently at V.T.O.S. When she finishes she will take on the world.

Cyril Fenlon was born and raised in Enniscorthy. He loves sport, especially soccer and supports Enniscorthy United who he used to play with. He wishes happiness to all.

E. Ryan grew up in Wexford town and enjoyed doing summer work from the age of ten. He likes to write about things that have disappeared from life today. He liked the old style pubs and shops.

E.C. has one brother and one sister. His mother is alive but his father passed away. He has seven county medals for playing rounders.

Gerald Morrin was born in Dublin in 1943. Reared on his uncle's farm, it was there he developed an interest in animals and agriculture. Always thought he would like to write but did not get round to it until relatively recently.

John Kehoe enjoyed science at school but now he likes reading, writing and history. His hobby is walking.

John Yates stopped writing in 1989 and only started again eighteen months ago. He's glad he did as it gives him enjoyment and pleasure.

Kirsten Sellhorn
Nothing can bring you serenity but yourself...

Kieran Sinnott is thirty-five years old and was born in Dublin. He lived and worked in England for five years. He now lives in Wexford.

Larry Connick
My name is Larry Connick and I have an interesting history.

Lillian McLoughlin is a Limerick woman. She loves creative writing because there can be funny twists at the end of the tale.

Michael Carroll is very interested in computers but likes creative writing as well. Sport is his big hobby and his favourite soccer team is Manchester United.

Michelle Cullen
I try to be friendly. I try to be optimistic. I try not to judge.

Martin Freeman was born in Crossabeg. He has three brothers and four sisters. He enjoys writing and self-expression and would like to see everybody else expressing themselves also.

Margaret Kehoe comes from Camolin. She likes television and reading. She admires the people who write for television. In her own way, she likes to write too.

Michael Bolger always considered that honesty is the best policy and his honesty is the most important thing for him. He always tries to tell the truth to the people he loves.

Michael Kinsella comes from Balliniry, Duncannon. He loves painting and writing and he sings the odd song.

Moira Naessens is forty-six years of age and works in Killagoley Training & Activation Centre.

Maureen O'Connor lives in the centre of Enniscorthy. She was born on December 2nd 1962. Her writing is all about her history.

Mary B. Keyes was born and raised in County Wexford, the sunny South East. She enjoys creative writing.

Noel Galavan has lived in Wexford all his life. He likes the beauty of nature and enjoys the process of writing.

Orla Slevin lives on a farm with her mother and father and her sisters.

Paddy Galvin lives in Oylgate where he stood for mayor and was chosen. He was very honoured to do this job.

Philip Priestly attends K.T.A.C. and is from Enniscorthy.

Pat Rossiter was born in Gorey in 1951. *Upward Decline* was his first collection of poems. Some of his poetry was previously published in The Wexford People, The Irish Independent, The Wicklow People and Good News for Youth magazine.

Sarah Tuomey lives on a farm way down the country, in Co. Wexford, a couple of miles outside Gorey. She has three brothers, two sisters and an elderly mother.

Tony Allen is originally from Dublin and moved to Wexford twelve years ago when he made Enniscorthy his home. He lives and works here now and all his friends are here.

Tom Lawlor is the second youngest of nine children. All the family are grown up now and his mother and father are deceased. He enjoys doing the writing class.

William Colfer started school at five years of age. He grew up with five brothers and three sisters. He liked the outdoor life but went to work in Dublin and then England. He is back here in Wexford since 1976.

William Doyle learned about music in St. Peter's College. He played rugby for Wexford Wanderers and Landsdowne Road. He likes to write about his past.

William Hayden hailed from Kilrush. He was an exceptionally talented visual artist with a unique, unmistakeable style. Gentle and enthusiastic, he participated in the creative writing workshops with great gusto and thoughtful energy.